Lemonade

It's so hot today.
I could drink a gallon of lemonade.

I could drink it all by myself.

Here comes my friend.
I will share my lemonade with her.

4

We can each have a half gallon of lemonade.

Here come two more friends.
We can share our lemonade with them.

We can each have a quart of lemonade.

Here come four more friends.
We can share our lemonade with them too.

We can each have a pint of lemonade.

Here come eight more friends.
We can share our lemonade with them too.

We can each have a cup of lemonade.

Wait! I have an idea!

It's so hot today.
Let's go swimming first!

I'll pour the sixteen cups back into the gallon jar.

14

I'll keep it cold while we swim.

How about that!
We still have a gallon of lemonade!